Nocturnal Animals

Wombats

Kristin Petrie
ABDO Publishing Company

visit us at
www.abdopublishing.com

Published by ABDO Publishing Company, 8000 West 78th Street, Edina, Minnesota 55439.
Copyright © 2010 by Abdo Consulting Group, Inc. International copyrights reserved in all
countries. No part of this book may be reproduced in any form without written permission from the
publisher. The Checkerboard Library™ is a trademark and logo of ABDO Publishing Company.

Printed in the United States of America, North Mankato, Minnesota.
082009
012010

 PRINTED ON RECYCLED PAPER

Cover Photo: Getty Images
Interior Photos: Alamy pp. 6, 12, 17; Animals Animals p. 10; Getty Images p. 1;
    iStockphoto pp. 7, 16, 18; National Geographic Image Collection p. 13; Peter Arnold pp. 5, 14,
    19, 21; Photo Researchers p. 8

Series Coordinator: Megan M. Gunderson
Editors: Megan M. Gunderson, BreAnn Rumsch
Art Direction & Cover Design: Neil Klinepier

Library of Congress Cataloging-in-Publication Data

Petrie, Kristin, 1970-
  Wombats / Kristin Petrie.
     p. cm. -- (Nocturnal animals)
  Includes index.
  ISBN 978-1-60453-740-6
  1. Wombats--Juvenile literature. I. Title.
  QL737.M39P48 2010
  599.2'4--dc22
                                                        2009025658

Contents

Wombats

What animal is nicknamed "bulldozer of the **bush**"? This furry creature is Australia's largest burrowing animal. It's the wombat!

Wombats are marsupials, like kangaroos and koalas. Marsupials are mammals that give birth to underdeveloped young. The young usually finish developing in the mother's pouch. Within the marsupial group, the wombat belongs to the order Diprotodontia. All diprotodonts have at least four **incisors**.

Three wombat species belong to the family **Vombatidae**. The southern hairy-nosed wombat is called *Lasiorhinus latifrons*. The northern hairy-nosed wombat is called *Lasiorhinus krefftii*.

The common wombat is named *Vombatus ursinus*. *Ursinus* means "bearlike." You may even think wombats look like your favorite teddy bear! Keep reading to learn more about this powerful, burrowing creature.

Nocturnal, Diurnal, or Crepuscular?

One way scientists group animals is by when they are most active. Nocturnal animals work and play during the night and sleep during the day. Diurnal animals are the opposite. They rest at night and are active during the day. Crepuscular animals are most active at twilight. This includes the time just before sunrise or just after sunset.

Scientists use a method called scientific classification to sort organisms into groups. The basic classification system includes eight groups. In descending order, they are domain, kingdom, phylum, class, order, family, genus, and species.

Built for Digging

Wombats are stout creatures with thick necks and strong shoulders. The three wombat species vary slightly in size. The largest wombats may weigh up to 88 pounds (40 kg). All three species are around 3.3 feet (1 m) in length. They are about 1 foot (.3 m) tall.

The wombat's strong claws are made for digging!

Wombat fur color varies from dark brown to cream. Yet a burrowing wombat's true color may be hidden by dirt! The common wombat's fur is coarse and has long **guard hairs**. Hairy-nosed wombats have silkier fur.

A wombat is faster than it looks!

A wombat's head features small eyes and short ears. The hairy-nosed wombat's nose is hairy! The common wombat's nose is big, bare, and black. Long, sensitive whiskers stick out from the common wombat's **muzzle**.

The wombat moves about on its four short legs. These end in wide, flat paws with strong claws. The wombat has a wobbly walk but is surprisingly fast. It can run nearly 25 miles per hour (40 km/h) over short distances! It can also swim.

Burrowing Down

Wombats are native to Australia. The common wombat lives in southeastern Australia, including Tasmania and nearby Flinders Island. It prefers **temperate** forests and coastal areas with a **humid** climate.

The hairy-nosed wombat has adapted to drier climates. The southern hairy-nosed wombat lives in southern Australia. Its **habitat** includes **semiarid grassland** and open woodland. The northern hairy-nosed wombat lives in open eucalyptus forests in central Queensland.

All wombats live in burrows underground. They use their strong limbs to dig into and sweep away soil. To enlarge a tunnel, a wombat rolls onto its back and scratches at the walls.

Wombats use minor burrows to escape danger and medium burrows for resting. Major burrows have sleeping chambers, branching tunnels, and numerous entrances.

A major burrow can be more than 100 feet (30 m) long!

N
W · E
S

GREENLAND

NORTH
AMERICA

ASIA

EUROPE

AFRICA

SOUTH
AMERICA

AUSTRALIA

Where Southern Hairy-Nosed
Wombats Live

Where Northern Hairy-Nosed
Wombats Live

Where Common
Wombats Live

Northern
Territory

Western
Australia

Queensland

South Australia

New South
Wales

Victoria

DETAIL RANGE MAP

Tasmania

Awake at Night

Wombats are nocturnal animals. In their burrows, they sleep through the heat of the day. The weather affects what time wombats leave their burrows. In summer, they may wait until after midnight. In winter, wombats may venture out in the afternoon.

Once awake, wombats usually spend time grazing. They eat while walking slowly with their noses to the ground.

Many nocturnal animals have special eye features. These help them find food and sense danger in the dark.

Often, wombats sleep on their backs with their feet in the air!

However, wombats rely on their other senses far more than on their small eyes. Wombats have excellent senses of smell and hearing. They also sense vibrations in the ground.

Nocturnal Eyes

Some lucky nocturnal animals have special eye features that help them in the dark. They may have large eyes compared to their body size. Also, their pupils may open wider than ours do in low light. These two features allow more light to enter their eyes.

After light enters an eye's pupil, the lens focuses it on the retina. In the retina, two special kinds of cells receive the light. These are rods and cones.

Rods work in low light. They detect size, shape, and brightness. Cones work in bright light. They detect color and details. Nocturnal animals often have many more rods than cones.

Many nocturnal eyes also have a tapetum lucidum behind the retina. The tapetum is like a mirror. Light bounces off of it and back through the retina a second time. This gives the light another chance to strike the rods. The reflected light then continues back out through the pupil. This causes the glowing eyes you may see at night!

NIGHT ANIMAL

DAY ANIMAL

RETINA

RETINA

RODS

CONES

TAPETUM LUCIDUM

RETINA

LENS

PUPIL

ANIMAL'S EYE (side view)

Plants Only!

Wombats leave their burrows when it is not too hot, cold, or dry outside. They often spend several hours searching for food. All wombats are herbivores. They eat grasses, fungi, herbs, mosses, and roots. Wombats get most of the water they need from these foods.

A wombat's diet depends on its **habitat** and the season. In areas that receive snow, a wombat will dig under it to find food. If

Wombats will drink water, especially if available plants get too

drought or fire destroys food sources, the wombat will adapt its diet. It uses its digging skills to unearth plant roots.

Roots and grasses are tough foods to rip and chew. The wombat's teeth grow continuously to make up for this wear and tear. Gnawing on hard roots and tree bark also helps keep teeth the right length.

Wombats have two upper and two lower incisors. These sharp front teeth help cut food.

Joeys

Wombat mothers are very protective of their young.

Scientists are still learning about wombat reproduction.
Hairy-nosed wombats are ready to bear young at age three.
Common wombats can reproduce a year earlier.

Like many marsupials, wombats start their lives in a special way. A female common wombat gives birth just 20 to 30 days after mating.

The baby wombat, or joey, is not fully developed. However, it does have claws and strong front limbs. The joey uses these to quickly crawl into its mother's pouch.

Safely inside the pouch, the joey nurses and grows. By four months, its eyes open and it begins growing fur. Next, its teeth begin to show. At six months, the joey begins peeking out of the pouch.

After about seven months, the joey occasionally leaves its mother's pouch. This only happens inside the burrow. And, the joey maintains contact with its mother. By eight months, the joey will move short distances from her. It also practices digging and scraping at the burrow walls.

By 18 months, the wombat is independent. The oldest common wombat in **captivity** lived to 26 years. In the wild, wombats probably live more than ten years.

Danger Down Under

Wombats have few natural enemies. Large birds such as eagles and owls may prey on unprotected joeys. Dingoes and foxes occasionally attack wombats, too.

A wombat's large size, powerful jaws, and escape burrows help it stay safe. And its short, stubby tail leaves nothing for predators to grab on to. If chased into a burrow, a wombat may use its body as a weapon. It can crush a predator against the wall!

Dingoes are wild dogs that are native to Australia.

Humans remain the wombat's main enemy. More than 200 years ago, European settlers brought livestock and other animals to Australia. These animals competed with the wombat for its grassy food.

People have also introduced foreign plants into wombat **habitats**. For example, buffel grass now grows in the northern hairy-nosed wombat's range. Buffel grass is not a healthy food source for wombats. And, it leaves less room for traditional foods.

In some areas, common wombats are considered pests. Livestock can step in burrows and break their legs. And if wombats burrow under fences, the tunnels can allow other pests into farming areas. So, farmers in parts of Victoria are allowed to kill wombats on their land.

Humans may threaten the wombat, but they also work to protect it. In some zoos, people can get very close to wombats. This helps people learn more about these fascinating creatures!

In Australia, road signs warn drivers to watch for wombats.

Deforestation presents another threat to wombat populations. Removing trees can affect their normal food supplies. This practice may also put wombats in closer contact with farmers.

Today, wombats are often killed by cars. When new roads are built, wombats do not change their nightly habits and routes. They are also attracted to lush roadside grasses.

Natural disasters such as floods, **droughts**, and fires also threaten wombats. Floods are a serious danger to burrowing animals. They can fill burrows with water quickly and without warning. Wombats may become trapped and drown.

Droughts can destroy a wombat's food supply. Long periods without water cause plants to shrivel up and die. This can affect reproduction rates and lead to starvation.

Fires are another frequent danger in the **bush**. In dry conditions, fires start easily and spread quickly. Wombats may hide safely in their burrows. Yet, the flames consume their grassy food. Many wombats and their **habitats** were affected by the 2009 Australian wildfires.

A healthy habitat is vital to the wombat's survival!

Looking Forward

At this time, the common and southern hairy-nosed wombats are not **endangered**. Yet food loss, disease, natural disasters, and predators threaten individuals. And, the southern hairy-nosed wombat's reproduction rate drops during **drought**.

The northern hairy-nosed wombat is more at risk. In the 1980s, just 30 to 40 of these wombats existed. So today, many **conservation** efforts are in place.

Currently, northern hairy-nosed wombats live only in Epping Forest National Park in Queensland. Cattle and dingoes are kept from their territory. And, a fence surrounds the entire population. Now, 115 northern hairy-nosed wombats are known to exist. And, scientists hope to establish additional populations.

Today, wombats are protected almost everywhere in Australia. Education about their endangered standing will help keep them safe. That way, the "bulldozer of the **bush**" will remain a fascinating wild Australian creature!

Scientists are working hard to protect the northern hairy-nosed wombat from extinction.

Glossary

bush - a large stretch of uncleared or mostly unsettled land covered with shrubby growth, especially in Australia.

captivity - the state of being captured and held against one's will.

conservation - the planned management of natural resources to protect them from damage or destruction.

drought (DROWT) - a long period of dry weather.

endangered - in danger of becoming extinct.

grassland - land on which the main plants are grasses.

guard hair - one of the long, coarse hairs that protects a mammal's undercoat.

habitat - a place where a living thing is naturally found.

humid - having moisture or dampness in the air.

incisor (ihn-SEYE-zuhr) - a front tooth, usually adapted for cutting.

muzzle - an animal's nose and jaws.

semiarid - having very little rainfall.

temperate - having neither very hot nor very cold weather.

Vombatidae (vahm-BAD-uh-dee) - the scientific name for the wombat family. Members of this family are closely related to koalas. The family includes three wombat species.

Web Sites

To learn more about wombats, visit ABDO Publishing Company on the World Wide Web at **www.abdopublishing.com**. Web sites about wombats are featured on our Book Links page. The links are routinely monitored and updated to provide the most current information available.

Index